12 ADVENTURES
ON NEW STATE LANDS
EXPLORING THE FINCH, PRUYN TRACTS

BY PHIL BROWN

 An ADIRONDACK EXPLORER Guidebook

Boreas Ponds looking toward the High Peaks. PHOTO: CARL HEILMAN II

THANK YOU TO OUR UNDERWRITERS:
William Gundry Broughton Charitable Private Foundation
Furthermore: a program of the J.M. Kaplan Fund

Published by ADIRONDACK EXPLORER
36 Church Street, Saranac Lake, NY 12983
AdirondackExplorer.org
& LOST POND PRESS
LostPondPress.com

Cover Photo: OK Slip Falls, by Nancie Battaglia
Back Cover Photo: Boreas Ponds, by Carl Heilman II
Maps by Nancy Bernstein • Book Design by Susan Bibeau
ISBN: 978-0-9903090-4-8

Foreword

We at the *Adirondack Explorer* believe that the Adirondack Park is one of the most beautiful places on the planet. That's why our newsmagazine focuses on ways to protect and enjoy it. We hope this guidebook will lead to adventures that will enhance your appreciation of this marvelous place.

Although I wrote the book, many others had a hand in its production. Susan Bibeau designed the covers and inside pages. Nancy Bernstein drew all the maps by hand. Several photographers, including Nancie Battaglia and Carl Heilman II, contributed color photos. I want to thank *Explorer* Publisher Tom Woodman, Associate Publisher Betsy Dirnberger, and Connie Prickett of the Nature Conservancy for reading my copy and fact checking. Thanks also to Dick Beamish, the founder of the *Explorer*.

If you're unfamiliar with the *Explorer*, please take the time to check it out. We are a nonprofit newsmagazine that publishes six issues a year in addition to an annual Outings Guide. For Adirondack aficionados, it is essential reading. Find out more at AdirondackExplorer.org.

Enjoy the outings!

—Phil Brown, Editor
Adirondack Explorer

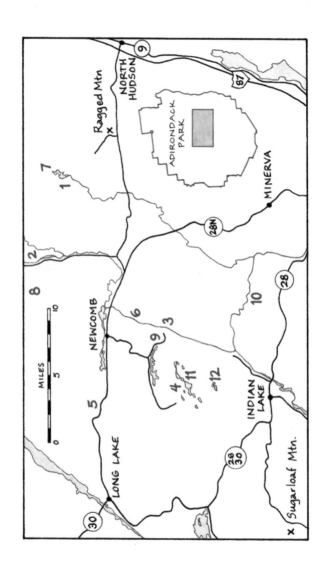

CONTENTS:

Introduction

In 2007, the Adirondack chapter of the Nature Conservancy stunned and elated wilderness lovers when it announced that it had purchased all 161,000 acres owned by Finch, Pruyn & Company, one of the biggest landowners in the Adirondack Park.

The scope of the deal was breathtaking. Finch, Pruyn owned vast tracts of forestland in the heart of the Park, including such natural jewels as Boreas Ponds, OK Slip Falls, the Essex Chain Lakes, and parts of the Hudson Gorge.

In the ensuing years, the Nature Conservancy worked out a plan for the future of the Finch lands. About 92,000 acres were sold to a pension fund as a timberland investment. New York State holds a conservation easement on these lands that allows responsible logging but prohibits subdivision and development. Most of the rest, some 65,000 acres, were sold to New York State outright and added to the Forest Preserve. As part of the Preserve, these lands are open to the public and will be kept forever wild.

The Nature Conservancy and Governor Andrew Cuomo deserve our gratitude for this milestone in the history of Adirondack conservation.

The *Adirondack Explorer* newsmagazine covered in detail the unfolding of the Finch, Pruyn deal from its inception: the acquisitions themselves, which took place over several years; the decisions, often controversial, on how the lands should be managed; and the recreational opportunities. The *Explorer* conceived *12 Adventures on New State Lands* with two aims in mind. First, to commemorate a blockbuster deal that will protect some of the most significant wilderness in the Adirondacks, providing habitat for a variety of wildlife and recreation for us humans. Second, to let people know what they can do on these spectacular additions to the Forest Preserve.

The former Finch lands offer something for everyone: the paddler, the hiker, the mountain biker, the cross-country skier, the trail runner, the rock climber. This book reflects that diversity of recreation and so is a departure from the *Explorer*'s earlier guidebooks, which focused on hiking. Of course, most trails lend themselves to multiple uses. They can be hiked, skied, run, and (if regulations allow) biked.

Because these lands were acquired by the state only recently, the state Department of Environmental Conservation is still working on management plans and creating amenities such as carry trails, campsites, and put-ins. Also, a lawsuit brought by environmentalists could change what's allowed in the Essex Chain Lakes region. *The descriptions in the book reflect facts on the ground in 2016. Check the DEC website for updates.*

Although these are day trips, don't treat them lightly. Whenever you enter the wilderness, you should be prepared in case someone turns an ankle or worse. This means carrying the Ten Essentials. The classic list is as follows: map, compass, sunglasses and sunscreen, extra clothing, headlamp or flashlight, first-aid

> **The state Department of Environmental Conservation's emergency hotline is 518-891-0235.**

kit, fire-starter, matches, knife, and extra food. It's also wise to carry an emergency shelter such as a space blanket, a lightweight tent, or just a large trash bag. If you have a cell phone, bring it for emergencies, but be aware that it may not pick up a signal in the wild.

The Adirondack Park contains 2.6 million acres of Forest Preserve, with thousands of miles of trails, thousands of miles of streams and rivers, and thousands of ponds. We hope this book will inspire you to support the Nature Conservancy's work and to discover more of the Adirondacks. You also might want to join the Adirondack Mountain Club (ADK) and to subscribe to the *Adirondack Explorer*. For more information, visit their websites: www.nature.org/adirondacks, www.adk.org, and www.adirondackexplorer.org.

If you are venturing into other parts of the Park, you may want to pick up the *Adirondack Explorer*'s other guidebooks: *12 Short Hikes Near Lake Placid, 12 Short Hikes Near Old Forge* and *12 Short Hikes Near Keene Valley*.

Happy adventures!

1 Boreas Ponds

Up to five miles of paddling with spectacular views of the High Peaks, plus side trips on LaBier Flow and the Boreas River. Carry: 3.1 or 3.6 miles.

Finch, Pruyn could have put a corporate retreat on any of its various tracts scattered throughout the Adirondack Park, but the timber company chose to build it at Boreas Ponds. It was an obvious choice: the ponds offer a magnificent view of the High Peaks.

The lodge was torn down four months after the state purchased Boreas Ponds in 2016, but the view hasn't changed, making the waterway a first-class destination for paddlers. Of course, the ponds also are a great destination for backpackers.

Boreas Ponds is reached via Gulf Brook Road, a former logging road. As this book went to press, the public was allowed to drive 3.2 miles up the dirt road. This meant paddlers had to carry or wheel their boats 2.5 miles to a put-in at LaBier Flow, an impoundment on the Boreas River. It's possible that more of the road will be open to vehicles in the future. Check the state Department of Environmental Conservation's website for updates.

The Boreas River and Boreas Ponds are named after the Greek god of the north wind.

Gulf Brook Road crosses LaBier Flow at the impoundment dam. If you're hiking, follow dirt roads another mile or so to Boreas Ponds (see map). If you're paddling, cross the dam and scramble down the bank to the water for an easy put-in. The flow is relatively short and much of it quite shallow. Once on the water, you'll enjoy great views of Boreas Mountain to the northeast and, after rounding a bend, the High Peaks to the north.

In a third of a mile or so, the waterway starts to narrow, with boulders poking up above the surface or lurking just

For canoeists willing to portage, Boreas Ponds is a delight.

below. If you bear right, the flow soon morphs into a real river and becomes too rocky to paddle. The state may build a canoe carry from the river to the ponds. In the meantime, it's easier to take out on the flow's northwest shore (see map). From there it's just 20 yards to the road. Once back on the road, you face a half-mile portage to a dam that raised the water level of the ponds. There is a good put-in just before the dam.

As the eagle flies, the ponds are only a mile and a half long, but if you do a circuit close to the shore, you can get in more than five miles of paddling. In addition, you can paddle up the inlet more than a half-mile if the water is high enough.

Boreas Ponds is a single water body, but before the dam was built (originally for logging) there were three ponds connected by marshy streams. Now lobes of the enlarged waterway, these are still called First, Second, and Third pond.

Each lobe is different, so it's like getting three ponds in one.

We'll describe a clockwise circuit. From the put-in, you have a direct view of Boreas Mountain. Shortly, you round a bend and take in a High Peaks vista that includes Mount Marcy and the Great Range. Other High Peaks that can be seen include Allen, Dix, and Sawteeth.

Hugging the shore, you come to a channel between the mainland and a wooded island; follow it to Second Pond, by far the largest of the three lobes. On Second, you pass by a forest of snags, ghostly trees that must have died when the dam flooded their ground. The pond also features a cluster of bog islands with carnivorous pitcher plants, leatherleaf, cotton grass, and the pink blossoms of bog laurel.

Not far from a humongous boulder rising out of the water, veer left into a wide channel that leads to Third Pond, the smallest lobe. Third Pond has a sickle-shaped archipelago of bog islands. A narrow bay in the northeast corner leads to the inlet, the Boreas River, which enters the pond by a culvert. Take out here, cross the road, and put in a stillwater on the other side. Don't be discouraged by the boulders and snags. Once you get past them, you'll be paddling up a wild and twisting river.

After exploring the river, return to continue your circuit of the ponds, now following the east shore. You'll pass a number of other islands and enjoy new views of the surrounding peaks. With any luck, you'll be in the company of loons.

DIRECTIONS: From Northway Exit 29, drive west on County 84 (also known as the Blue Ridge Road or Boreas Road) for 7.1 miles to Gulf Brook Road on the right. Drive 3.2 miles up the dirt road to a large parking area before a vehicle barrier. The road is not plowed in winter and may be closed during the spring mud season. **N43° 58.8672', W73° 54.0242'**

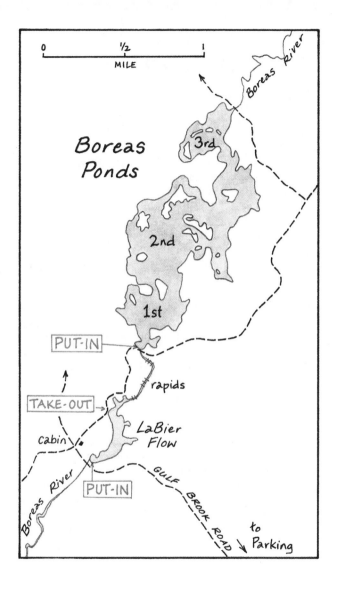

2 Hudson & Opalescent Rivers

Up to nine miles of paddling on two placid rivers on the edge of the High Peaks. No carries.

The Opalescent River is one of the wildest rivers in the Adirondacks, arising on the north slope of Mount Marcy and flowing into the Hudson River near Tahawus. With the state's purchase of the MacIntyre East tract, including many miles of riverfront, paddlers now have easy access to both the Opalescent and the upper Hudson.

We'll describe an end-to-end trip that begins and finishes on the Hudson, with a side trip up the Opalescent. If you don't have a second car, you'll need to bicycle or walk three miles back to the put-in. We'll also suggest an option for a round trip that doesn't involve a shuttle.

Teddy Roosevelt, then vice president, was relaxing at Lake Tear of the Clouds, the highest source of the Hudson, when he learned President McKinley lay dying.

The most convenient put-in is at the County Route 76 bridge over the Hudson. This is the road that leads to the former iron and titanium mine at Tahawus. The takeout for this trip is a bit tricky. You want to exit someplace where the river comes close to County Route 25. Follow the directions below, find a good takeout, and mark the spot (temporarily) so you'll recognize it from the water.

From the put-in, start paddling downstream. At first, the river is not that attractive as waste rock from the mine covers the left bank. In less than a half-mile, you leave the industrial blight behind and soon enter a wider stretch of river known as Sanford Lake. This shallow, marshy water offers views of Santanoni Peak to the northwest and the cliffs on Wallface to the north.

At the confluence of the Hudson and Opalescent. PHOTO: SETH JONES

After passing through Sanford Lake, the river narrows again. A half-mile later, at 2.2 miles from the put-in, you reach the mouth of the Opalescent on the left. How far you go up the Opalescent will depend on the water levels and your tolerance for paddling against the current. You'll have to contend with shallow riffles in places. That said, it's often possible to go two miles or more up the river.

The Opalescent is wonderfully twisty, with a new vista around every bend. Perhaps the best views, to the east, are of Allen Mountain, one of the Adirondack High Peaks. The sandbars on the curves serve as delightful beaches for pic-

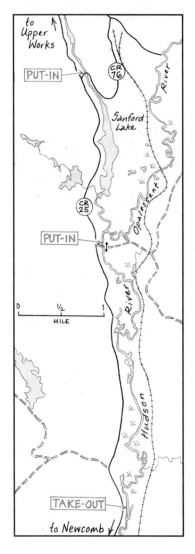

nicking, swimming, or just lounging. Landing on the shores would have been illegal before the state bought MacIntyre East from the Nature Conservancy.

At 1.7 miles up the Opalescent, you pass under a trestle for a rail line that leads to the old mine. Whether you turn around here or push farther, you'll enjoy a leisurely downstream cruise on your way back to the Hudson.

Less than a quartermile below the confluence, you come to a logging-road bridge over the Hudson. This was part of the MacIntyre East purchase. Since the bridge is just a few yards from Route 25, it is a convenient place to launch a canoe or kayak. If you prefer to do a round trip, put in here, paddle upriver to Sanford Lake and then paddle up the

Opalescent. The bridge also serves as an alternative takeout if you want a shorter end-to-end trip.

Whatever trip you decide on, we recommend exploring the river below the logging bridge—assuming you don't mind paddling against the current on the way back. You'll enjoy a wilder stretch of water as the Hudson pulls away from the road. About two-thirds of a mile downriver from the bridge, a large alder marsh affords a spectacular view of Algonquin Peak and Mount Colden. This is a good turnaround spot if you're heading back to the bridge.

About 1.25 miles past the marsh, you reach a sizable backwater on the right between the main river and the road. It's worth poking around in here for gorgeous views of the High Peaks, including Mount Marcy, the state's highest summit.

Just downriver of the backwater, you'll find solid ground on the right bank. Presumably, you have left your second car or a bicycle somewhere in the vicinity and marked the spot. The bank is likely to be somewhat steep, but it's a very short distance to the highway.

TAKEOUT: From Northway Exit 29, drive 17.6 miles west on County Route 84 (Boreas Road or Blue Ridge Road) to County 25, which leads to Tahawus. Turn right and go 3.4 miles to a yellow traffic sign warning of a curvy road. Mark your takeout somewhere nearby and continue to the put-in.

PUT-IN: Continue another 3.0 miles to the junction with County 76. The bridge over the Hudson is a stone's throw from the intersection. **N44° 02.641', W74° 03.467'**

ALTERNATIVE PUT-IN: If you plan a round trip from the logging-road bridge, the directions are simpler. From the junction of County 84 and County 25, drive north on County 25 for 4.4 miles. The bridge is visible on the right. **N44° 00.952', W74° 03.284'**

ɜ Blackwell Stillwater

Six miles of paddling on a quiet stretch of the Hudson, with a short trip up the Goodnow River. Carry: 0.3 miles.

The Blackwell Stillwater is a wide, placid piece of the Hudson River that can be paddled in a morning or afternoon, featuring nice views of Polaris Mountain, a visit to the site of an old logging dam, and a side trip up the Goodnow River. It's a worthy alternative or complement to paddling the nearby Essex Chain Lakes.

The trip begins with a 0.3-mile carry to the river from a parking area on Drakes Mill Road, one of many old logging roads in the Essex Chain region. The dirt road leads to an iron bridge built by Finch, Pruyn in 1992 to access timberlands on the east side of the Hudson. Just before the bridge, a short trail on the right leads to the water.

If you intend to paddle the Hudson north of the bridge and explore the Goodnow, we recommend you *not* take this trail. Instead, look for a grassy trail on the left that leads to a put-in north of the bridge. By starting here, you avoid an upstream paddle through a riffle beneath the bridge.

A river driver once drowned on Blackwell Stillwater while conducting logs down the river. A cross carved in a white pine by one of his co-workers can still be seen.

As you travel upriver, look for the Goodnow, which enters the Hudson on the left a few hundred feet from the put-in. The mouth is fairly broad and marshy. You can't go far up the Goodnow before encountering beaver dams, but it's worth poking around this seldom-visited stream. Also, the view on the way back of Polaris Mountain with the river in the foreground is a keeper.

The side trip up the Goodnow River is short but sweet. PHOTO: PHIL BROWN

From the Goodnow, you can continue up the Hudson for more than a half-mile before reaching rapids, at which point you can turn around and enjoy a leisurely trip downstream. The river is bordered on both sides by state-owned Forest Preserve: there is no sign of civilization until you get to the iron bridge.

The short, shallow riffle under the bridge is easily manageable when paddling with the current (assuming sufficient water to cover rocks). Over the next half-mile or so, you may see some hunting camps built by the Polaris Mountain Club on the east shore. The owners enjoy exclusive rights to one-acre parcels around the camps until October 1, 2018. The structures are to be dismantled after that date.

Before and after the bridge, the Blackwell Stillwater is quite broad, perhaps 200 feet across. Usually, the woods come right down to the shore, but you pass marshes and alder swamps as well. The biggest marsh is on the east side, roughly a mile and a half from the bridge, near the outlet of Cheney Pond. As you pass this marsh, you'll see a channel that can be paddled a short way.

About two miles from the bridge, you come to the site of a dam built in the 1800s. Finch, Pruyn would store logs on the impounded water and then flush them downriver in the spring. Today, the dam is little more than a collection of large boulders.

Be aware that the current quickens as you approach the site. A bedrock ledge on the right shore is an excellent picnic spot, but getting to it is tricky. Because of the rapids, it's difficult to land your boat near the ledge. A safer option is to take out in a small cove on the right and bushwhack the short distance to the ledge. You may spot an old sluice channel on the edge of the cove.

The ledge offers a fine view of the Hudson looking north, bordered by dark evergreens. The music of rushing water adds to the wild ambience. This is a wonderful spot to enjoy lunch or just rest before turning back. On the return trip, the current poses no trouble. As you approach the iron bridge, look for the carry trail on its downstream side and exit there. If you explore the Hudson above and below the bridge and poke around the Goodnow, you can get in about six miles of paddling.

DIRECTIONS: From NY 28N in Newcomb, about 0.5 miles west of the Newcomb Town Hall, turn south on the west end of Pine Tree Road (a short loop road), then turn onto Goodnow Flow Road. Go 4.3 miles to a junction with Woody's Road. Bearing left, continue 1.4 miles to the dirt Chain Lakes Road. Turn left and go 2.7 miles to a kiosk and barrier. To reach the Hudson, carry around the barrier and down the road for 0.3 miles. Depending on where you put in, look for paths on the left or right shortly before the iron bridge. Either leads to the river. **N43° 53.7164', W74° 10.0880'**

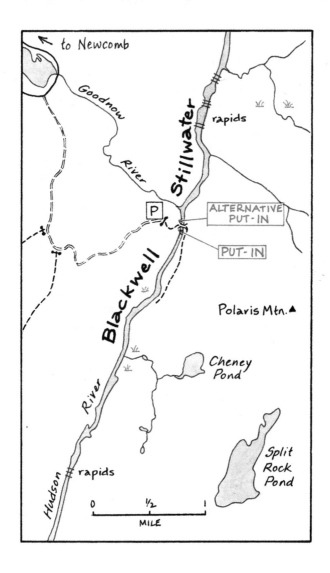

4 Essex Chain Lakes

Ten miles of paddling on eight pristine ponds, with side trips possible.
Three carries totaling about a mile.

The Essex Chain Lakes are a paddler's dream: eight connected ponds surrounded by pristine forested peaks. It's no wonder that the parking lot was full on the morning the state opened the lakes to the public for the first time in the fall of 2013.

The Essex Chain and nearby ponds offer so much paddling that you may want to camp out or make two day trips.

For most people, the journey will begin at the parking area north of Deer Pond. However, the disabled may obtain a permit from the Adirondack Interpretive Center in Newcomb (518-582-2000) to park near the causeway between Fourth and Fifth lakes, all but eliminating the carry.

The Gooley Club on Third Lake traced its roots to the Chain Lake Sportsman's Camp in the late 1800s.

From the register, carry your boat 0.25 miles to Deer Pond, following a dirt road most of the way and then turning right onto a very short path that leads to the north shore.

The paddle across Deer Pond is only a tenth of a mile (though the pond is worth exploring if you have time). After landing, you face a 0.5-mile carry to Third Lake. Follow a trail to a dirt road, turn right, and follow the road 0.35 miles, then follow carry-trail markers to the lake's north shore.

At 262 acres, Third Lake is the largest water body in the Essex Chain. From the middle of the lake, you enjoy views of some of the larger peaks in the region, such as Fishing Brook Mountain to the northwest and Vanderwhacker Mountain to the east. You may see loons on this lake.

The put-in on the north shore of Third Lake. PHOTO: NANCIE BATTAGLIA

Paddle south a third of a mile to a wide channel that leads to Second Lake and then angle southwest to a carry trail to First Lake that follows the left bank of the outlet. The paddle from the Third Lake put-in to the takeout is about 0.7 miles. The carry is only a tenth of a mile, leading around rapids.

First is one of the bigger lakes in the Essex Chain, and floatplanes are allowed to land and take off here. Paddle along the north shore to the outlet. The marshy, twisty stream is one of the highlights of the trip. How far you go downstream will depend on water levels and your tolerance for pulling over beaver dams. If you're willing to pull over one or two, you may be able to travel three quarters of a mile.

After turning around, retrace your route to Third Lake to explore the rest of the Essex Chain. As you paddle east, toward Fourth Lake, you'll notice an island on the right. Behind it is a large bay where the Gooley Club built its quarters. The club must vacate its buildings by October 1, 2018.

Until then, the members have exclusive rights to one-acre parcels around the structures, so be sure not to trespass. The buildings eventually will be torn down.

After passing the island, you reach Third's inlet, a sluggish stream that winds through a marsh to Fourth Lake. You may see red-winged blackbirds and other birds in the wetland. Fourth Lake is less than a half-mile long and can be crossed in a matter of minutes. You leave the lake via "the tube"—a big culvert beneath an old logging road. The state plans to replace the culvert with a bridge.

You emerge from the tube onto Fifth Lake. Follow the right shore. In a half-mile or so, you reach the shallow inlet. In low water, you may have to meander around patches of mud and push your way through lilypads. After a third of a mile on the stream, you reach Sixth Lake.

Sixth is shaped like a boomerang, curving to the right. As you round the bend, you enter a wide channel that leads to Seventh Lake. The channel is so broad that it's hard to tell where one lake ends and the other begins. Traversing the two lakes requires paddling only three quarters of a mile.

The inlet of Seventh Lake can be found on the south shore. The stream is not navigable, but the state plans to create a short carry trail to Eighth Lake, the last lake in the Essex Chain. Until then, the inlet is a good place to turn around. The state also plans to build a carry trail from Third Lake to Jackson Pond. There already is a 0.4-mile carry trail from the north shore of First Lake to Grassy Pond.

DIRECTIONS: From NY 28N, about 0.5 miles west of the Newcomb Town Hall, turn south on the west end of Pine Tree Road (a short loop road), then turn onto Goodnow Flow Road. Go 4.3 miles on Goodnow Flow Road to a junction with Woody's Road. Turn right onto Woody's Road and go 1.5 miles to Cornell Road. Bear left and go another 4.4 miles to the parking area. After the turn onto Woody's Road, most of the driving will be on dirt roads. The roads are often rocky. **N43° 53.294', W74° 15.879'**

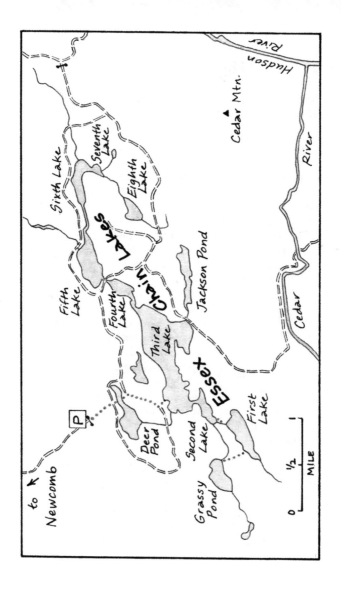

5 County Line Flow

Up to five miles of paddling across a small lake and up a wild brook, with nice views. Very short carry.

This outing differs from the other paddling trips in this guidebook in that County Line Flow lies on privately owned conservation-easement lands, not in the public Forest Preserve. This doesn't make the waterway any less charming, but it does mean the visitor must abide by a few special rules as the state owns only limited recreational rights.

As its name suggests, County Line Flow lies near the border of Hamilton and Essex counties, between Newcomb and Long Lake. The put-in on the south shore is reached by a very short carry on a good path.

Except at the put-in, the public is not allowed to step on the shore of the flow. However, much of this trip—perhaps the best part—takes place on the inlet, Fishing Brook, where it is permissible to get out of your boat so long as you stay within 33 feet of the water. Fishing is allowed on both the flow and the stream, but hunting, trapping, and camping are prohibited.

> Fishing Brook is one of 350 streams in the state with public easements that allow people to fish on private land.

From the put-in follow the south shore to a marsh at the west end of County Line Flow and look for the inlet near a large beaver lodge. As you cross the flow, you'll enjoy views of Kempshall Mountain to the northwest and Goodnow Mountain to the southeast. Goodnow is recognizable by the fire tower on its summit. The fire tower on Kempshall, which overlooks Long Lake, was taken down in 1977.

You might want to meander among the lily pads and ex-

Though wide at first, Fishing Brook narrows upstream. PHOTO: LISA GODFREY

plore the grassy channels of the marsh before heading up Fishing Brook. You're likely to hear the basso croaks of bullfrogs and the chatter of red-winged blackbirds.

Fishing Brook enters the flow at the north end of the marsh. It's possible to paddle more than a mile up the brook before encountering a pair of large beaver dams. There is little current. The brook starts out fairly wide but gets more narrow and twisty as you travel upstream. The scenery varies from marsh to evergreen corridor to alder thickets.

About 0.8 miles from the flow, you come to a logging-road bridge, which can be used as an alternative put-in or take-out. It's located on Pickwacket Pond Road less than a mile from State Route 28N. Although the dirt road lies on easement lands, the public can drive to the bridge.

Just after passing under the bridge, you reach one of the best views of the trip: a watery bend dotted with lily pads and bordered by swaying grasses with 3,346-foot Kempshall rising in the distance. In season, you'll see an abundance of blue flag, a wild iris, in the immediate vicinity.

You'll likely have to paddle over or around a few beaver dams as you meander upstream through the alders. At 1.2 miles from the flow, you come to two bigger dams, one just beyond the other. This is a good turnaround, but hard-core paddlers may want to try to push farther. Keep in mind that paddling conditions could change, depending on water level and beaver activity.

The return to the flow is a leisurely paddle. Once there, you can paddle along the flow's north shore. As you approach the east end of the water body, you may spy a camp through the trees. This is owned by the Kempshall Mountain Club, which leases land from the property owner.

Be aware that there is a spillway dam at the end of the flow. There is current here, so steer clear as you make a circuit of the flow. (Below the spillway, Fishing Brook is shallow and rocky.) To return to the put-in, paddle around a small island and then follow the south shore. The trip up Fishing Brook and the loop around the mile-long flow will give you nearly five miles of paddling.

County Line Flow's proximity to Route 28N means you can hear passing vehicles. Although the road is not busy, some paddlers may find the occasional noise a distraction. Of course, its nearness to the road also may be seen as a convenience.

DIRECTIONS: From the junction of NY 28N and NY 30 in Long Lake, drive north and east on NY 28N for 7.8 miles to the County Line Flow access road on the left. The parking area is at the end of the short road. If coming from Newcomb, the turn will be on the right about 5.9 miles west of the Newcomb Town Hall. **N43° 58.6279', W74° 16.5272'**

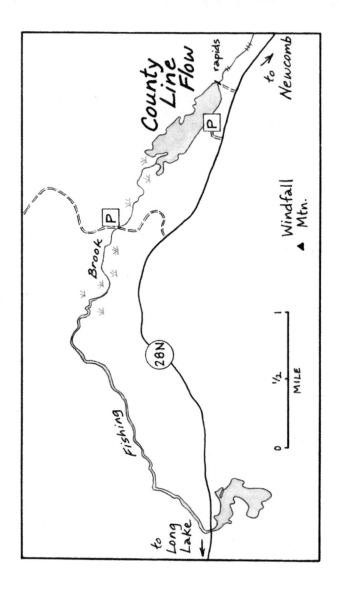

County Line Flow

rapids

to Newcomb

P

P

Brook

Windfall Mtn.

28N

½ MILE

0

Fishing

to Long Lake

6 Hudson Whitewater

A mild whitewater journey of 7.5 or 14.5 miles. Shuttle required.
Moderate carry at end. Carries around bigger rapids optional.

The Hudson Gorge has long been the scene of commercial rafting trips, but the rapids are so formidable that only expert paddlers—whether in raft, canoe, or kayak—dare to run them on their own. Fortunately for intermediate paddlers, the Finch, Pruyn deal opened up a tamer stretch of the Hudson River above the gorge.

This 12-mile length of the Hudson has plenty of exciting rapids, but they are more manageable than those in the gorge. Nevertheless, paddlers need whitewater skills. The trip will be easier in a ducky (a rubber kayak) rather than a canoe or standard kayak. Duckies are less likely to capsize if you hit a rock.

In the late 1960s, environmentalists thwarted a proposal to dam this stretch of the Hudson.

Check the river gage at North Creek (via USGS website) before setting out: for intermediate paddlers, a reading between 4.0 and 5.0 feet is desirable. Putting in at the Newcomb boat launch, paddlers can enjoy a 7.5-mile trip to the Blackwell Stillwater (see page 16) or a 14.5-mile trip to a takeout just before the confluence with the Indian River. Expert paddlers can continue through the Hudson Gorge to the hamlet of North River, a total of 30 miles or so. Note: check the gage early in the morning or late in the day when the water level is not affected by dam releases.

There are numerous rapids between Newcomb and the Indian River, with lazy stretches of river in between. Most of the rapids are class II (relatively easy), but the first two—Long Falls and Ord Falls—reach class III (moderately difficult). It's possible to carry around both on marked trails.

Canoeists approach a rapid below Ord Falls. PHOTO: NANCIE BATTAGLIA

From the Newcomb boat launch, paddle east on Harris Lake for a mile and enter the outlet. Shortly after, you come to the Hudson. Bear right to head downriver. In a quarter-mile, you pass under Route 28 (where there is a spot of quick water) and enter a broad marshy section of river with nice views of nearby mountains.

A mile from the highway, you reach Long Falls, which is a series of rapids, not a waterfall. They can be avoided by carrying for a third of a mile on the right bank. Maybe a mile farther on is Ord Falls, another series of rapids and the heaviest whitewater on the trip. Again, these can be avoided by carrying for a half-mile on the right bank.

Below Ord Falls, you encounter several smaller rapids on the way to Blackwell Stillwater, which is reached after passing an island. You may want to scout some of the rapids.

The Goodnow River enters from the right shortly before

a former logging bridge over the Hudson. There is a bit of quick water beneath the bridge. The takeout for the shorter trip is on the right immediately afterward. It's a 0.3-mile carry to the parking area.

Placid water extends nearly two miles downriver from the bridge. You then come to the site of a 19th-century logging dam, which is now just a collection of boulders, followed by the first of nine rapids before the takeout. You should scout the drop below the dam.

About 1.3 miles farther on, the Cedar River enters from the right. In another 2.3 miles, you reach a takeout on the right bank, marked by a large sign. Don't miss it! If you go too far you'll be heading into the Hudson Gorge. The carry from the river to the road is less than a tenth of a mile. It's another 0.2 miles to the parking area.

Getting back to your starting point will require a shuttle. If you take out at Blackwell Stillwater, the drive back to the put-in is about 20 minutes. If you take out at the Indian River, it's about an hour. You can hire an outfitter to do the shuttle for you.

FIRST TAKEOUT: From NY 28N, about 0.5 miles west of the Newcomb Town Hall, turn south on the west end of Pine Tree Road (a short loop road), then turn onto Goodnow Flow Road. Turn left and go 5.7 miles to Chain Lakes Road. Turn left and go 2.7 miles to a kiosk and barrier.
N43° 53.7164', W74° 10.0880'

SECOND TAKEOUT: From the intersection of NY 28 and NY 30 in Indian Lake, drive east on NY 28 for 1.3 miles to Chain Lakes Road on the left, just before Lake Abanakee. Drive 3.9 miles down this road to the vehicle barrier at the former site of the Outer Gooley Club.
N43° 49.6599', W74° 12.0512'

PUT-IN: From the Newcomb Town Hall on NY 28N, drive east 0.7 miles to Lake Harris Road on the left. Just after turning, you'll see the boat launch on the right. **N43° 58.2694', W74° 08.7489'**

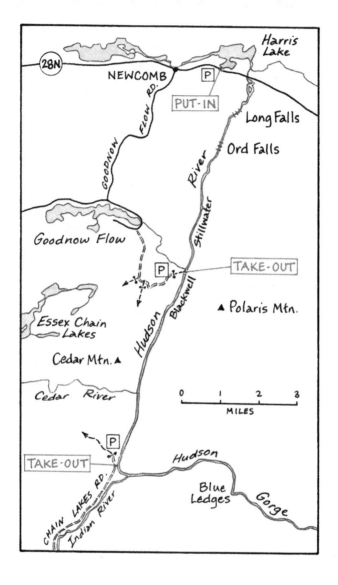

7 Boreas River Headwaters

Mountain-bike ride of 3.6 miles to Boreas Ponds, followed by 4-mile hike on easy logging roads to beautiful headwater pond.

Though now one water body, Boreas Ponds used to be three small ponds on the Boreas River. A logging dam raised the water, merging the ponds and creating a sizable lake. If you're visiting the ponds without a canoe, hiking to the beautiful headwaters of the Boreas River north of the ponds is a worthy outing.

When this book went to press, the state had yet to mark trails or install trail signs on the Boreas Ponds Tract. This outing is straightforward enough that if you follow our directions, you shouldn't get lost. It combines mountain biking and hiking on easy-to-follow logging roads.

> The log cabin just uphill from LaBier Flow was built in the early 1890s.

Under the state's interim-access plan for the tract, the public is allowed to drive up the dirt Gulf Brook Road to a gravel lot located 3.6 miles from Boreas Ponds. The plan also lets people ride mountain bikes from the lot to the ponds but no farther. Be aware that the access rules may change. Check the state Department of Environmental Conservation website for updates.

The road is easy biking (or hiking), with a few small hills. At 2.6 miles, you reach LaBier Flow, an impounded section of the Boreas with a view of Boreas Mountain and some of the High Peaks. Just beyond, you reach an intersection. Turn right and pedal another mile to the Boreas Ponds dam.

The dam offers a nice view through a strait toward the Great Range. Broader views can be enjoyed from the site of a lodge that was demolished in the summer of 2016. The state

The Boreas River begins at this pond. PHOTO: PHIL BROWN

closed the site to allow it to reseed, but eventually it will be open to the public. Once that occurs, you can go there by walking back a hundred feet and turning right onto a short road. Take in as many scenes as you can because you won't see the ponds again.

From the dam, you follow logging roads for four miles to the Boreas headwater pond. The roads are in good shape and allow fast, easy hiking. If you normally hike two miles an hour, you may be able to hike three miles an hour. As you hike, you'll enjoy the shade of an overarching canopy most of the way and, in season, the chatter of woodland birds. You'll also see occasional disturbances from past logging operations, such as gravel pits, skidder roads, and clearings.

For the first three miles, stay on the same road. You'll pass side roads on the right at 0.15 miles and 1.3 miles from the dam. The second is reached just after crossing Snyder Brook on a bridge. At 1.75 miles, you reach a fork with another good road. The way left leads in 0.9 miles to the northern tip of Boreas Ponds. To reach the headwater, however, continue straight here.

At 3.0 miles, you come to another junction with another good road. This time, turn left. As you start downhill, you should follow a compass bearing of roughly 340 degrees (assuming your compass is adjusted for true north).

The road has several bends, but it generally heads west and northwest. Whereas the first road traverses a typical Adirondack forest with lots of hardwoods, this road passes through a spruce-fir forest, lowland boreal habitat. There is no canopy, so wear a hat and bring sunblock. You will have occasional views of the North River Mountains and Allen Mountain, one of the High Peaks. Look for moose tracks; they show up well in the road's loamy surface.

At 4.0 miles from the dam, you come to a lovely pond where the Boreas River begins its long journey to the Hudson River, though here it is a mere trickle. The divide between the Hudson and Lake Champlain watersheds lies less than a quarter-mile north of the pond. The waters on the other side feed the Ausable Lakes.

The old road notwithstanding, the pond sits in a wild landscape rarely visited by people. The southern end of the Colvin Range is visible to the northeast. Mount Marcy and Mount Haystack, two of our tallest peaks, can be seen toward the north peeking over the treetops.

If you follow the road past the pond, it soon peters out amid brush and saplings, but looking back you'll have a good view of Boreas Mountain.

DIRECTIONS: From Northway Exit 29, drive west on County 84 (also known as the Blue Ridge Road or Boreas Road) for 7.1 miles to Gulf Brook Road on the right. Drive 3.2 miles up the dirt road to a large gravel lot before a vehicle barrier. **N43° 58.8672', W73° 54.0242'**

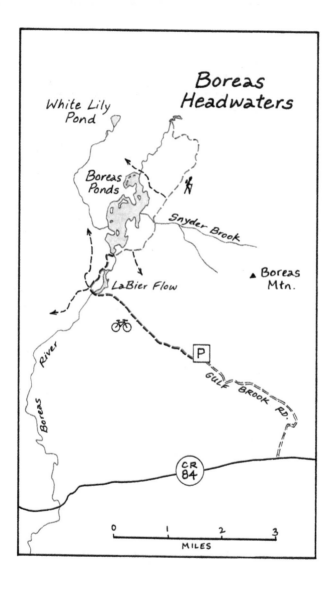

Boreas Headwaters

White Lily Pond

Boreas Ponds

Snyder Brook

Boreas Mtn.

LaBier Flow

Boreas River

GULF BROOK RD.

P

CR 84

0   1   2   3
MILES

8 Lake Andrew

A 4.7-mile hike mostly on old logging roads to a pristine pond, with views of Santanoni and other peaks. Also a good early-season ski.

Lying a few miles southeast of Santanoni Peak, Lake Andrew is a worthy destination for a hiker, trail runner, or cross-country skier. It's the centerpiece of MacIntyre West, a 5,770-acre tract formerly owned by Finch, Pruyn and sold to the state by the Nature Conservancy in 2014.

Most of the route to Lake Andrew follows former logging roads, so you can make good time. The roads are ideal for jogging or skiing. Since you gain 630 feet in the 4.7 miles to the lake, the return trip is especially fun on skis. Given Lake Andrew's remoteness, however, be prepared to break trail on the way in.

The parking area for Lake Andrew is off the Tahawus Road in the town of Newcomb. It's the same parking area used by hikers going to Bradley Pond or Santanoni Peak. You begin on a logging road shared by these hikers. At first, it's marked by blue disks.

The name Santanoni is thought to reflect the Abenaki pronunciation of "Saint Anthony."

At 1.1 miles, the road crosses a wetland with a view north of the High Peaks Wilderness. Soon after, you can glimpse the Twin Slides through the trees—the first of many views of these bedrock scars on the east slope of 4,607-foot Santanoni.

After 1.8 miles, the road reaches a junction with the foot trail to Bradley Pond and the Santanoni Range. Most hikers turn right to head down the trail. Those going to Lake Andrew, however, continue on the road. Beyond here, there are no blue disks to mark the way.

About 100 yards beyond the junction, the road crosses a

The wild lake sits below Mount Andrew.

large tributary to Santanoni Brook, which flows into Henderson Lake, the source of the Hudson River. The road parallels the stream for a good while. At 2.2 miles, it crosses into the MacIntyre West tract. Up to this point, you have been traveling through privately owned conservation easement lands.

A bit past the Forest Preserve boundary, you reach a junction with another road that veers right and up a hill. Bear left here, continuing to walk beside the stream.

Almost three miles from the trailhead, the road passes a hunting camp, one of many on the MacIntyre West tract. The camps must be vacated by October 1, 2018. Until then, stay away from the buildings. The owners have exclusive rights to one-acre parcels around the camps.

After passing this camp, the road dips and then resumes climbing. At 3.3 miles it reaches a T-intersection near a cluster of camps. Turn left. You come to another junction at 3.6 miles. Make a sharp left here. Up until now you have been traveling primarily west or southwest. After the turn, you are going southeast.

As you head down this road, you pass more camps. Make sure to turn around for a great view of the Twin Slides on Santanoni. The graded logging road comes to an abrupt end at 4.0 miles. Look for a rough skid road on the right and follow it uphill. After crossing three bridges, you enter a small clearing at 4.2 miles. You'll see two trails, one going straight, the other going right. Take the first one. Shortly you reach a wider trail, which may be muddy. Turn left. At 4.7 miles, look for a short path on the left leading to the shore of Lake Andrew.

Sitting at the foot of 3,081-foot Mount Andrew, the lake has a wild feel despite a hunting camp on the opposite shore. Once the camp is dismantled, it will be even wilder, a nice spot to relax and swim in summer.

On the return trip, you might want to take a detour to a clearing with an outstanding view of Santanoni Peak—better than any enjoyed on the way to the lake. When you reach the T-intersection mentioned earlier, bear left instead of right. This road bends left and then climbs gradually to the clearing. After enjoying the vista, retrace your steps to the T-intersection and back to the car. The detour adds a mile to the round trip.

Because the logging roads are smooth, they require only a few inches of snow to be skiable. Keep Lake Andrew (or the clearing) in mind for an early-season ski tour. If there isn't much snow, you may have to walk the rougher trails at the end.

DIRECTIONS: From Northway Exit 29, drive west on County Route 84 for 17.9 miles to County Route 25 (the Tahawus Road). Take a right and go 6.4 miles to a junction. Turn left to stay on County 25 and go 2.0 miles to a trailhead sign on the left. Turn here for the parking area.
N44° 04.149', W74° 03.691'

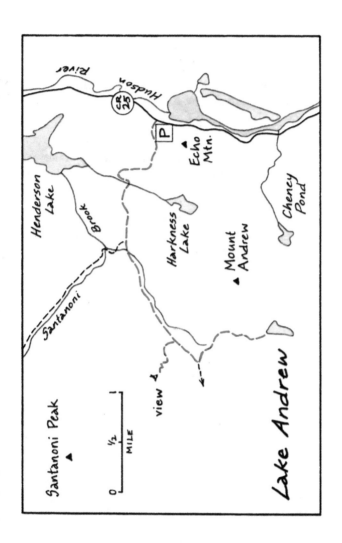

9 Upper Hudson Ski Loop

An easy 4.2-mile cross-country-ski trip or hike with opportunities for viewing two Adirondack rivers.

After purchasing the Essex Chain Lakes tract, the state established the Upper Hudson Ski Loop on old logging roads and ATV trails south of the hamlet of Newcomb. For the most part, the trails are wide, smooth, and gentle in grade, suitable for intermediate skiers and even novices capable of controlling their speed on the short downhills.

Of course, the trails also can be snowshoed in winter and hiked in other seasons, and their smooth surface makes them ideal for trail running. Mountain biking is not allowed. Since the state designed the loop with cross-country skiing in mind, we'll describe the excursion as a ski tour.

The 4.2-mile lollipop loop lies near the confluence of the Hudson and Goodnow rivers, at different times paralleling one or the other of the rivers. When this guidebook was published, the state was planning to build other ski trails to connect the loop with Newcomb hamlet.

> The Goodnow River is named after Sylvester Goodnow, who settled in the Newcomb area in 1820.

The Goodnow River begins at Goodnow Pond, courses south to Goodnow Flow, and then flows southeast to the Hudson. The parking area for the Upper Hudson Ski Loop is on Goodnow Flow Road a bit north of where the river leaves the flow.

From the parking area, you ski a hundred yards along a trail that parallels the road. It leads to a former logging road. Turn left and ski up the logging road. You soon come to a register.

This section of trail is flat, sitting on a ridge high above

The trails can also be hiked on all fours.

the Goodnow River. Although you can hear rushing water, glimpses of the river are few and far between. A half-mile beyond the register, the trail splits. This is the start of the loop proper. The state recommends people ski in a counter-clockwise direction as it's deemed easier that way.

Bearing right at the junction, you enjoy a gentle down-hill glide past a beaver meadow, followed by a short climb. At the height of land, you face the most difficult downhill in the loop: the trail descends in two pitches almost to the Goodnow River. Given good snow conditions, the descent will seem tame to an intermediate skier.

At the bottom of the hill, the trail turns left and parallels the river. You can catch only fleeting glimpses of the water through the trees, but you can leave the trail for a closer look.

About two miles into the trip, the trail begins to parallel

the Hudson. As you ski, you can see the river clearly through the trees, but you might want to head off trail through the open woods for a better view. If you get close enough, you can find nice views up and down the river.

At 2.75 miles, the trail bends left and pulls away from the river. At this point, you are quite close to a slough on the Hudson that affords an impressive vista looking upstream. It's worth getting off the trail for a gander.

The trail then climbs 250 yards to an obvious logging road. Although you turn left to stay on the loop, some skiers may first opt to go right to enjoy a short, easy descent along the road. It leads to an old bridge over a creek. The road continues on the other side but is overgrown.

Back to the junction: the road climbs easily to a pull-off with perhaps the best view of the surrounding terrain. Through the bare hardwoods of winter you can see the Hudson below and a number of peaks in the distance, including Polaris Mountain and 3,385-foot Vanderwhacker Mountain. In summer, much of the view is obscured by leaves.

A quarter-mile past the pull-off, the trail starts to level. Skiing along the flats, you'll pass two other logging roads entering from the right. These are brushy but can be explored if you want to extend the trip. After the second logging road, a short downhill brings you back to the junction where the trail splits. Follow your tracks back to the car.

DIRECTIONS: From NY 28N, about 0.5 miles west of the Newcomb Town Hall, turn south on Pine Tree Road (a short loop road), then turn onto Goodnow Flow Road. Go 4.3 miles to a junction, bearing left to stay on Goodnow Flow Road. Continue 1.1 miles to a parking area on the left, just before the bridge over the Goodnow River.
N43° 54.9192', W74° 11.1451'

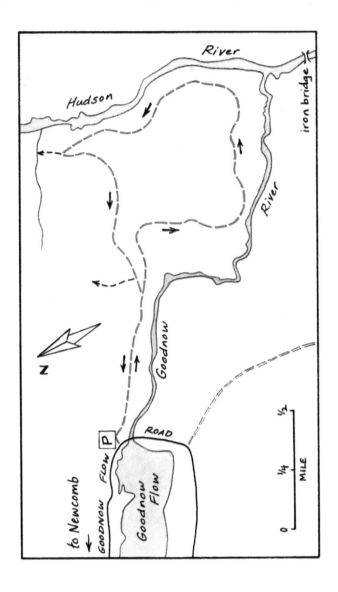

River

Hudson

iron bridge

River

Goodnow

N

P

ROAD

GOODNOW FLOW

Goodnow Flow

to Newcomb

½

¼

MILE

0

10 OK Slip Falls

Three-mile hike to one of the Adirondack Park's iconic waterfalls. Outing can be extended with hike to Hudson River.

One of the largest waterfalls in the Adirondack Park, OK Slip Falls had attained near-mythical status when it was owned by Finch, Pruyn and thus off limits to the public. We've heard that people occasionally risked a trespass ticket to get a look at the hidden jewel.

Today, hikers can see the falls legally by following a 3-mile trail to a ledge that looks across a gorge at the 250-foot waterfall—truly one of the natural landmarks of the Adirondacks.

The trail starts on the north side of Route 28 between the hamlets of North Creek and Indian Lake. At first, you follow a pre-existing trail that leads to Ross, Whortleberry, and Big Bad Luck ponds. Marked by red disks, this trail passes through a handsome forest and is easy to follow, though there is a muddy patch near the beginning.

In the old days, loggers yelled "OK slip!" as a warning when releasing logs from OK Slip Pond into a wooden flume that carried them toward the Hudson River.

At 0.8 miles, before reaching the ponds, you come to a junction with a new trail that leads to OK Slip Falls. Turn right here and follow the blue disks.

No trees needed to be cut for the new trail. It winds through the woods with gentle ups and downs. About three-quarters of a mile from the turn, after crossing a stream and passing through a hemlock grove, you can see an old beaver pond on the right. It has mostly drained, leaving behind a wet meadow.

In another 0.6 miles—or 2.2 miles from the original trailhead—you reach a dirt road that goes to the Northern Frontier Camp, a privately owned boys camp on OK Slip Pond.

OK Slip is one of the largest cascades in the Adirondacks. PHOTO: NANCIE BATTAGLIA

Turn left and follow the road for 250 feet to a junction with an old woods road. Turn right at the sign and head down the old road, which is now overgrown.

After a half-mile or so (2.8 miles total), the trail veers left off the old woods road and then descends in two short switchbacks to an overlook with a spectacular view of the falls. There is a second overlook 75 feet beyond the first. The drop-off from either lookout is precipitous, so adults should keep a close eye on young children.

As you gaze across the gorge, OK Slip Brook slides off a bedrock shelf, plunging amid evergreens in a silver ribbon and sending up clouds of mist.

For most hikers, the sight of OK Slip Falls probably is satisfying enough, but you can extend the outing by taking another trail to the Hudson River. It adds about two miles to the round trip.

You will have passed the start of the trail to the river just before reaching the overlooks. On the way back, turn right for the side trip. Marked by blue disks, the trail soon crosses a footbridge over OK Slip Brook. From the bridge, you can watch the flowing water disappear over the ledge at the crown of the falls. On the far side of the brook, the trail climbs for a quarter-mile before descending steeply to the Hudson. It ends just upriver from OK Slip Rapids. In season, you may see the colorful rafts of commercial outfitters taking clients through the Hudson Gorge.

OK Slip Falls also is a good destination in winter. The trail to the lookouts can be hiked easily on snowshoes. With enough snow, it could be skied without much trouble. Of course, a skier would need to be extra careful near the ledges. Ice climbers sometimes ascend the frozen falls. Don Mellor, the author of *Blue Lines: An Adirondack Ice Climber's Guide,* says the climb is only moderate in technical difficulty, but he warns that the ice may be unstable.

OK Slip Falls is part of the Hudson Gorge Wilderness Area. Wilderness regulations do not allow the use of mountain bikes.

DIRECTIONS: From the junction of NY 28 and NY 28N in North Creek, drive west on NY 28 for 10.1 miles to a parking area on the left near the start of a local road. If coming from the west, the parking area will be on the right 7.6 miles past the NY 28/NY30 junction in Indian Lake. From the parking area, walk west along the highway for two-tenths of a mile. The trail is on the opposite side of the road. **N43° 46.3366', W74° 07.7787'**

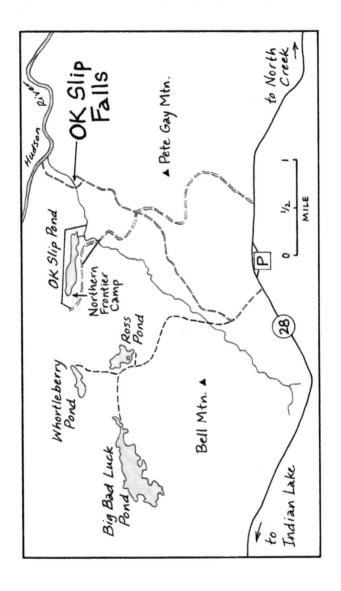

11 Essex Chain Biking

A 10-mile mountain-bike ride on old logging roads that takes you through the woods to pristine ponds.

Although the Essex Chain Lakes are known primarily as a paddling destination, the state has opened many miles of former logging roads in the vicinity to mountain biking. It's a different way to see the ponds and woods and enjoy some cycling away from vehicle traffic.

The dirt roads—mostly smooth and easy to ride, though with some hills—are in the Essex Chain Lakes Primitive Area, but they connect to other old logging roads in the region. Thus, it's possible to pedal 30 miles or more. We'll describe a roughly 10-mile trip that takes in many of the region's scenic highlights.

Start at the Deer Pond parking area used by paddlers. From the register, coast downhill for a few hundred yards to a junction. Turn right here to make a 2.8-mile loop around Deer Pond. You'll be able to glimpse Deer Pond through the trees, but there will be opportunities later for better views.

> Some environmentalists objected to the decision to allow bikes in the Essex Chain Primitive Area.

Sections of the road around Deer are sandy, but if you persevere, the traction improves. At 2.3 miles from the register, after passing a large beaver pond, you come to a carry trail on the right that leads to Third Lake, the largest water body in the Essex Chain. Bikes are not allowed on the carry trail, so dismount and walk the short distance to the lake's north shore. The view is well worth the small effort.

At 2.9 miles, you reach a T-intersection with the road you started on. Turn right and go about a mile (with a few ups

The Essex Chain roads were built for logging vehicles. PHOTO: LISA GODFREY

and downs) to a causeway between Fourth and Fifth lakes, with views of low peaks on the horizon. Since this is one of the more scenic spots on the trip, it's worth stopping to rest. Just before the causeway there is a parking area for the disabled and an outhouse.

From the causeway, pedal uphill to another intersection, reached at 5.1 miles from the trailhead. If you turned right here, you would reach the Cedar River after several miles. The state plans to build a bridge over the Cedar. If it does, you could cross the river and visit Pine Lake (see page 52). For now, however, bear left at the intersection and continue 0.5 miles to a junction with a road on the right. Follow this road, which is in poorer shape, for 0.5 miles to Jackson Pond. This water body is large enough to attract loons, and it offers stellar views of Blue Mountain, about ten miles away in the west, as well as many other peaks.

After enjoying the scenery, head back to the main road and turn left to return to the parking area. On the way, you have two opportunities to see Deer Pond up close. When you reach the south terminus of the Deer Pond loop, continue straight but keep an eye out for a large outhouse on the left. Stop here and walk a short distance to a campsite and small dock at the eastern tip of Deer Pond. This vantage offers a vista of virtually the entire pond.

Resuming the ride back to the parking area, you soon pass a very short carry trail that leads to the north shore of Deer Pond and a different perspective of this pretty water body. The carry will be on the left just before the northern terminus of the Deer Pond loop. From there it's just a minute's ride back to the parking area.

The excursion could be greatly extended by riding to the iron bridge over the Hudson River after visiting Jackson Pond. (See map for the route.)

Although the lakes and ponds provide attractive scenery, the landscape still bears the scars of its logging past: gravel pits, clearings, grown-over skidder trails. In time, though, the woods will heal, the trees will grow bigger, and the canopy will arch over the roads.

DIRECTIONS: From NY 28N, about 0.5 miles west of the Newcomb Town Hall, turn south on the west end of Pine Tree Road (a short loop road), then turn onto Goodnow Flow Road. Go 4.3 miles on Goodnow Flow Road to a junction with Woody's Road. Turn right onto Woody's Road and go 1.5 miles to Cornell Road. Bear left and go another 4.4 miles to the parking area. After the turn onto Woody's Road, most of the driving will be on dirt roads. The roads are often rocky. **N43° 53.294', W74° 15.879'**

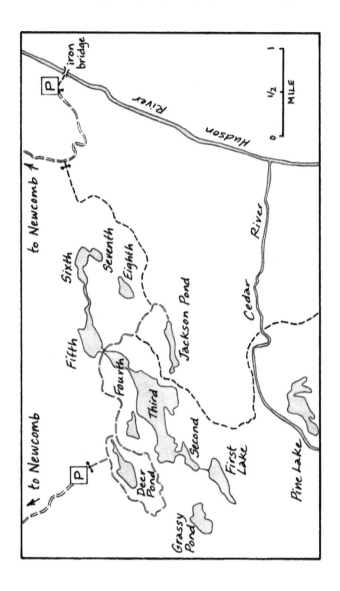

12 **Pine Lake**

A four-mile bike ride (or hike) on old logging roads to a gorgeous pond, with short detours to the Cedar River and a smaller pond.

When the state announced its plan to acquire 65,000 acres of former Finch, Pruyn land, most of the publicity went to such natural treasures as Boreas Ponds, Essex Chain Lakes, OK Slip Falls, and the Hudson Gorge. Pine Lake got lost in the media blitz.

That's a shame, because Pine Lake is a handsome body of water that, in another time, would have been a celebrated acquisition by itself. At more than 90 acres, it is one of the larger lakes in the region, with a beautiful evergreen shoreline.

The question is how to get there. Pine Lake can be reached by an easy four-mile hike (or trail run) along old logging roads, but since the roads are open to mountain bikes, many people will prefer to ride there. Overall, the road surface is fine for mountain bikes, but the cycling might be too hard for young children. There are sandy sections where it's difficult to get traction, and you must be prepared to ride up and down several hills.

In the late 1800s, Mike and Olive Gooley ran a boardinghouse in the building that became the headquarters of the Outer Gooley Club.

The outing can be extended with a short side trip to Clear Pond. However, bicycles are not allowed on the trail to the pond. If you're riding, you'll have to abandon your bike for a while.

The journey to Pine Lake begins at the former site of the Outer Gooley Club, reached by a dirt road from the hamlet of Indian Lake. A meadow near the parking area offers a view of the Hudson River. Sign in at the register just beyond

The trail ends at Pine Lake's northeast shore. PHOTO: NANCIE BATTAGLIA

a vehicle barrier (in big-game season, people are allowed to drive farther up the road).

The logging road is occasionally marked by blue disks. Beyond the register, it climbs to a junction at 0.65 miles, where another logging road comes in from the left. Continue straight here.

At 1.2 miles, you come to a trail on the left that leads to Clear Pond. If you take the side trip, you'll reach the south end of the pond in about 0.3 miles. Beavers have constructed a large dam across the outlet. On a clear day, the pond offers fine views of the small peaks to the north.

In another quarter-mile up the logging road, you arrive at a second vehicle barrier. This is as far as hunters are allowed to drive during big-game season, which begins in late October. The road then descends to Mud Pond, which is easily seen through the trees.

At 2.75 miles, you come to a major fork. The main road

bends right, but you want to go left. About a quarter-mile after the turn, look for a short footpath on the right that leads to a quiet stretch of the Cedar River. The state plans to build a bridge in this vicinity. Once constructed, it will allow people to bike or hike to the Essex Chain from Indian Lake (see page 48).

Continuing up the logging road, you'll soon enjoy another

PHOTO: NANCIE BATTAGLIA

view of the Cedar through the woods. At 3.9 miles, the road reaches Pine Lake. There is a fork here. If you go straight, you come to a campsite. We recommend turning right to enjoy a great view of the lake from the northeast shore. A nearby spit of bedrock is a fine place to take in the scenery, sunbathe, or eat lunch. If you're capable, you might want to swim to an islet about 50 yards offshore. It's mostly rock, with a couple of bushes.

Pine Lake is a wild place, but don't be surprised if you see a plane land or take off. Floatplane pilots are allowed to fly in clients who want to hunt, fish, and camp in the area.

In winter, snowshoers and cross-country skiers should be able to get to Pine Lake without difficulty. However, the access road is not plowed all the way to the former site of the Outer Gooley Club. Also, the state plans to designate the road to the Cedar as a snowmobile trail.

DIRECTIONS: From the intersection of NY 28 and NY 30 in Indian Lake, drive east on NY 28 for 1.3 miles to Chain Lakes Road on the left, just before Lake Abanakee. Drive 3.9 miles down this road to the vehicle barrier at the former site of the Outer Gooley Club. Be aware that the road turns to dirt after the first mile. **N43° 49.6599', W74° 12.0512'**

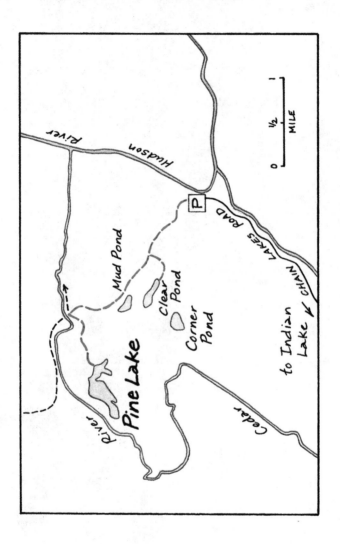

A climber on Kittens, Rainbows, and Lollipops.

Sugarloaf Mountain

Rising 450 feet, the cliffs on Sugarloaf Mountain tend to grab the attention of people driving down Cedar River Road, especially if those people are rock climbers. Since the state acquired land around the cliffs in April 2014, Sugarloaf has seen a fair amount of activity. The guidebook *Adirondack Rock* describes 18 routes, and the authors continue to post new routes on their website. The book rates the overall quality of the climbing at Sugarloaf as excellent (four stars out of a possible five). Although you may have to contend with dirt and moss at the start of a climb, the routes become considerably cleaner once they get above the trees.

Sugarloaf is especially appealing to those who enjoy slab climbing: the rock is relatively featureless, for the most part lacking cracks and holds. Climbers must rely on delicate balance and the friction of their soles to make their way upward.

> Anyone who climbs these cliffs should seek more information from the guidebook *Adirondack Rock* or AdirondackRock.com. Climbing is risky and should not be undertaken without proper equipment and training.

Most of the routes are considered moderate in difficulty. Eleven of those described in *Adirondack Rock* are graded 5.8 on the Yosemite Decimal System scale, which ranges from 5.0 (easy) to 5.15 (extremely difficult). The hardest routes at Sugarloaf are rated 5.10. Many of the routes are runout, providing few opportunities for placing gear to protect against a long fall.

For experts, perhaps the best route is Sole Fusion, which the guidebook awards five stars. It's 600 feet long, divided into five pitches. Three of the pitches are rated 5.10. "If you like friction, every pitch is superb. One of the best, long outings in the central Adirondacks, and a must-do for slab

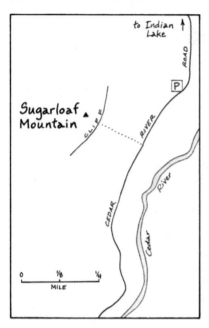

aficionados," *Adirondack Rock* says.

One of the best of the easier routes is Tier Pressure, which gets four stars. It's 420 feet long and divided into four pitches. The hardest pitch is rated 5.8+. The easiest route at Sugarloaf is Quarter Inch, which is rated 5.5. It gets no stars.

Climbers will be rewarded with impressive views of the wild lands to the south, including several peaks approaching 4,000 feet in height.

Steer clear of hunting camps. The owners have exclusive rights to one-acre parcels around the camps until October 1, 2018. The camps are to be dismantled after that date.

DIRECTIONS: From the intersection of NY 28 and NY 30 in the hamlet of Indian Lake, drive west on NY 28/30 for 2.1 miles to Cedar River Road and turn left. Drive 9.6 miles to a grassy pull-off on the right. Park here and walk about five minutes farther down the road to where it levels out. Turn off the road (heading right) and hike a few hundred yards to the cliff. Note: the road turns to dirt after 7.8 miles and beyond is usually closed until mid-May in spring. **N43° 45.3645', W74° 27.3319'**

Palm-O-Granite at Ragged Mountain is aptly named.

Ragged Mountain

The state acquired Ragged Mountain along with Boreas Ponds in April 2016. Within a few months, climbers had established nine routes, most of them hard. The *Adirondack Rock* website gives four out of five stars to Ragged for the overall quality of the climbing.

The routes range in difficulty from 5.3 to 5.13 on the Yosemite Decimal System scale. All but two are only one pitch.

One of the best moderate routes is Kittens, Rainbows, and Lollipops (rated 5.8), which climbs a corner crack to a small roof that must be circumvented. The website gives the route five stars and describes it as "simply awesome, one of the best single pitches of its grade in the park."

The Nature Conservancy
Adirondacks

pursue
adventure

support
conservation

Get more info: nature.org/adirondacks

Email: adirondacks@tnc.org

Call: 518-576-2082

Follow: @AdirondackTNC

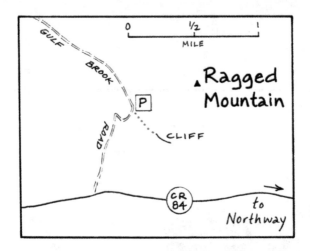

The website also gives five stars to Invasive Species, rated 5.10, and Runnin' Ragged, rated 5.11. The easiest route at Ragged, Stairway to Lichen (5.3), is two pitches and rates three stars.

Ragged offers splendid views to the south of peaks in the Hoffman Notch Wilderness.

The cliff is reached by a 0.25-mile herd path that starts 0.8 miles up the dirt Gulf Brook Road (which leads to Boreas Ponds). This section of the road was open to vehicles under the interim-access plan.

DIRECTIONS: From Northway (I-87) Exit 29, drive west on County 84 (also known as Blue Ridge Road or Boreas Road) for 7.1 miles to Gulf Brook Road on the right. Drive up the road 0.8 miles to an unmarked trail on the right. Look for the path just after you pass the second of two gravel pits on the left side of the road. The path heads southeast, crossing old skidder roads, and is sometimes hard to follow. It should become more defined with use. **N43° 57.852', W73° 51.948'**

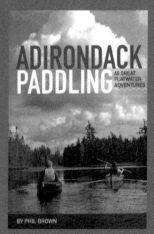
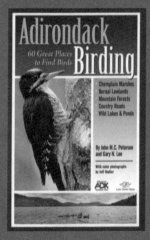